DIG FOR SURVIVAL

DIG FOR SURVIVAL

Self-sufficiency gardening
on allotments and small plots

PETER ELLIOTT

Drawings by Peter Foxwell

LUTTERWORTH PRESS
Richard Smart Publishing

First published 1976

Published by Lutterworth Press
Luke House, Farnham Road, Guildford, Surrey
and Richard Smart Publishing

Copyright © Peter Elliott, 1976

ISBN 0 7188 7001 8

Printed by Cox and Wyman Ltd
Fakenham, Norfolk

CONTENTS

I will subdue my conscience to the plot

Sheridan

1 BEGINNINGS

Dryden was, of course, talking about something else when he wrote 'Plots, true or false, are necessary things'. But the phrase, three hundred years later, still holds if it's applied to growing what you eat.

A vegetable garden—or more precisely in the context of this book, an allotment—is not the only answer to survival in these inflated mid-seventies. But it helps.

Thirty years ago 'Dig For Victory' was a wartime slogan and it is still remembered today; digging for survival needs to be taken no less seriously. What you produce yourself is something you've actually got and which you don't have to buy. You can also trade any surplus. The same economic simplicity is attached to North Sea Oil. Our allotment hasn't meant any reduction in my wife's housekeeping, but our domestic balance of payments isn't as bad as otherwise it might have been.

And the food is fresh and therefore tastes better.

And even if it didn't, the effort of providing it makes me think it tastes better.

And it's fun.

Well, no. Sometimes it's not fun; sometimes it's a long day's journey into the compost heap.

It's hard work, frustrating, maddening, tedious, boring: all of these things . . . sometimes.

But until the summer laziness sets in—something I'll touch on later—the body's fitter, the mind relaxed, the larder fuller and the purse at least stays heavier longer.

This book is not an instant crib towards a diploma in horticulture. Professional garden-writers will probably not approve of it, but it is no threat to their well-tended patch. It is not aimed at the good gardener who wants to become excellent, nor the gifted amateur who seeks perfection. It is not an encyclopaedia of horticulture, nor a tool or seedsman's catalogue, nor a definitive guide to growing anything.

It is aimed, rather, at the kind of man I was, when I began growing vegetables three or four years ago—basically an ignorant fool but hungry for better-tasting food, in greater quantity, and costing less. It is intended as a commonsense guide to getting the best you can from the land you've got according to your time, ability and eagerness. It is a collection of ideas based on how I have got away with it, or how some others I know have got away with it, and how you too can get away with it.

The book doesn't pretend to be exact, nor are its rules and guidelines universal, sacrosanct or even—always—thoroughly reliable. But they've worked for me, and if I correctly identify a trend I am a relatively early convert to a growing throng.

A recent trend? Actually, there is nothing new about allotments.

During the first war, there were a million and a half of them in Britain. During the second, around 2 million. The figure dropped away some years later, as affluence began to spread and people believed it really never had been so good. Now that idea has also dropped away and the figure's climbing again. Two years ago, there were 60,000 applications on the national waiting list for allotments and it's certainly bigger now.

Some councils have responded to this land hunger and have turned over more land to this use. But councils in many parts of the country still convert allotments to other things and still, taking over unused land, make it many times more available to other uses than for food. And the waste of national land is prodigious.

Official figures of derelict land list well under 150,000 acres. In fact, there is much, much more. The railways and trunk roads have thousands of miles of boundary land going to waste. How many electricity sub-stations have you seen which occupy a much larger, weed-ridden plot than the building itself apparently needs? Local authorities or private enterprise hold vast areas of land scheduled for some future use (perhaps years in the future) which in the meantime could grow something for somebody. One researcher recently calculated that there were some 10,000 acres of vacant derelict sites in London alone and that if even half of these were turned over to food production the result would be 100,000 tons of potatoes, nearly 100,000 tons of cabbage and over 150,000 tons of carrots. And that's *every year*. And that's also while thousands of acres of agricultural land are being lost each year to building, to roads, to industry, and while more than half of Britain's food comes in from abroad.

So badger your council, your local industries, the public corporations. And if, nowadays, there is increasing sympathy for squatters in long-empty houses, why not try squatting on land? At least you won't be harming it.

Commercial over.

Assuming you've got an allotment, how much time and effort are you prepared to put into it? It's something you should think about before starting out. I suspect (for it's certainly my experience) that it could be much less than the experts suggest. Twenty hours a week during the spring and summer, eight to ten a week during the autumn, and less during the winter? That's one professional estimate I have read. I believe you can get it down, quite effectively, to about ten or twelve hours in summer and five or six in the autumn.

The trouble is that allotments aren't, in general, just outside the back door. You can't occupy the five or ten minutes before tea, for example, in a quick survey, or weeding, or watering which, added up, can take a lot of the worst work out of growing. You will have to walk, or cycle, or drive to your allotment and this perhaps infrequently, and then feel you must spend at least two or three hours on it. And you will, usually, have other things to do with that time.

And yet . . . there is, as I've said, this great hunger.

The Chairman of one of Britain's big seed companies, Cuthbert's, identified the trend a couple of years ago. 'Gardening,' he said, 'is Britain's biggest leisure industry—it's not leisure, it's bloody hard work. It's a national mania.' He should know, for his company is thriving on the growth in sales of packets of seed. And his customers don't complain with a return of perhaps £30 or £40 worth of tomatoes, in greengrocer's terms, from an investment of around 20 pence.

And who are these customers, these gardeners, you?

A 1969 government committee on allotments, under the Chairmanship of Professor Harry Thorpe, suggested that more than 60 per cent of allotment holders were aged between 40 and 65, that almost half were manual workers, and that two in every ten were retired.

It's changed since then.

Young, or, at least, younger, people are now very much involved. The proportion of professional and sedentary workers involved is increasing. Lovers of good, fresh vegetables have found the best and cheapest way of getting them is by growing them. And more of them are growing, besides staple crops, precisely the kinds of things they can't normally find in shops, or won't normally buy in shops because of their price.

These growers are not persuaded by the pretentious renaming of the National Allotments and Gardens Society to the National Allotments and Leisure Gardens Society; allotments don't need their image refurbished, as that government committee urged. They are plain and simple plots for turning out good, cheap food.

There are still lots of old men, retired now, who spend several hours a day on their plots, and every day. Partly it's because they like it and have always done it, possibly because they've nothing much else to do.

The main thing is not to be put off by what they seem to achieve in this virtually full-time work. A man near me lives most of his days in a cage of netting, wire and posts up to seven feet high which must have cost a small fortune to erect. I've never seen his soil, because it's several inches below a thick carpet of straw and compost. Sometimes it's hard to see him, hidden in great forests of vegetation. He looks, and possibly is, miserable most of the time, fearful of some catastrophe. The only time he speaks to me is to snarl if I burn something instead of rotting it. But I refuse to be disheartened by his powders, fertilisers and sprays and I shall not cower before his monstrous-unwilting plants. I can get what *I* need with less time, cost and effort.

As often as these ancient mariners, you can also find solitary wives, putting in the odd hour in mid-morning or afternoon, while children are at school and husbands at work. They look good on it and cheerful about it, and they're usually quietly competent and successful. The other chief category of allotment gardeners is the relatively young couple, working together on some evenings. They tend to be as yet without children. It's significant that they're probably at this business because, on smaller, starting-out incomes, they can't afford not to be.

How much time and effort, then, is really needed? The answer is, whatever you can afford. Don't let your plot make you feel guilty. If it doesn't get enough of your time, you'll not get enough—or good enough—produce. Or you'll find you have a bitter backlog of work that will, in the end and at some season, have to be attacked in a blitzkrieg lasting several days.

Remember you don't need to be as perfect in approach as the professionals imply. Most of the time, you'll find, you can simply get away with it.

One cautionary note, however.

You can't fool the council all of the time.

It's true that you can get out of the ground what you put into it, but it's also true that you can get out of it a lot more, if you're lucky. The well-dug plot, according to the dominant school of gardening, rewards most and is safe. But weather, holidays, blight or bugs can ruin the best of plots. The quick corner-cutting gardener can pick up plenty of produce, given a certain consistency, but he too can get caught out by flood or drought, pulled muscles, a holiday at the wrong time and black-fly on his beans. And worst of all by the man from the council who gives him thirty days to clean his ground, tidy his paths, grow more food—or else.

So far, I've survived most of these hazards, and our stomachs, freezer and accounts have done well. And this is how.

2 DIG

You begin, of course, with the land.

Begin right at the beginning and find out, first, what kind of land it is. For years I was deterred by references to acid or alkaline soil, lime-loving and lime-hating plants, and so on. Like many others, I don't doubt, I even assumed that lime was acid, just because lime juice was. It's not, of course, in the gardening context.

There's no need to be deterred. Analyse the soil yourself.

And that's not as mysterious as it sounds. Simply go into a good chemist's, or gardening shop, and ask for a soil analysis kit. The instructions and operations are simple, the cost is little, and you'll know thereafter what you might have to do—or not do—about improving the land. An even simpler way, of course, is to ask your neighbours, or the allotment society which is almost certainly based on your site. It's unlikely that the nature of the soil will vary much from one site to another, although it is possible that you are inheriting a plot which has already had too much or too little of one kind of feeding.

It's doubtful whether you can have too much land, except in your capacity to work it. It's doubtful whether you'll be able to get enough, once the fever gets you. It's probable that you have, or can get, more than you think.

The size you get from your council will usually be measured in a five-rod or ten-rod strip. Even so, this can and should be complemented where possible by some output from your home. If you don't have a garden there, it's still remarkable what a start you can make from a few seed trays and an airing cupboard or central heating boiler, or a few pots, or even window boxes.

Even a carpet-sized garden at home can give you some fresh, seasonal vegetables. A five-rod plot could keep you out of the greengrocer's most of the summer. A ten-rodder can provide most of the vegetables an average family might want in a year.

Begin with the assumption that you're getting a new plot. Perversely, this probably means it's an old one—weed-ridden, grass-covered, lumpy and neglected. Actually, if it's not been worked for a year or two, it might be in basically good heart, but you're going to need a lot of determination and muscle to put it into shape.

If you can, take it in the autumn; you'll need time to rough it up and let the winter break it down for you. And if you can, without the council or your neighbours protesting, give it some drastic early treatment.

There are two quick ways of clearing badly overgrown land—chemically or by fire. If it's dry enough, and safe enough, burn it off. You'll have lost a potential compost material, but you'll soon make more, and some weeds need burning anyway.

Or what you can do is cover it with chemical.

Not, however, sodium chlorate. Certainly that will kill all the green stuff but it will also leave the ground sterile for six months to a year. And there are few things more depressing, as I found on taking over a plot where such had happened, than working land with virtually no heart and life left in it. I turned up fewer than a score of worms, when I first turned over that plot.

Weedol, which is a short-term plant destroyer killing only what it touches, is expensive; longer-lasting but not so destructive as sodium chlorate is Dalapon. Two weeks after its use, the roots of couch grass—for my labour, the allotment's worst nuisance—should be dead and ready for digging deep under. It's as well, incidentally, if you are using a chemical on long grass and weeds, to sickle them down first, for such a tangled mess is harder to clear when it's dead.

Very well. You now have a sort of crew-cut plot, and it's late autumn. There is no real—or, at least, immediate—alternative to the next step.

You are going to dig.

Actually, there is an alternative, strongly advocated by Dr. W. E. Shewell-Cooper and others, that you let the worms dig it for you. It's not an immediate solution, and I'll deal with it later.

At this stage, you do the digging.

There are three rules to remember.

Don't try to dig too much too quickly.

Don't dig up your sub-soil.

Don't dig with your back to the wind, unless you *want* aching kidneys.

On new (old) ground, you are wise to start with a spade. The fork is used later, for turning over reasonably cultivated land. Pick the spade you can handle comfortably and, if you can afford it, one made of stainless steel, which cuts more cleanly into and out of the ground with fewer clods sticking to it. If you're of limited stamina, a small edging or 'lady's' spade will serve you well. The man next to me, in his sixties and with not too robust a heart, worked over his plot far better than I, using only a small spade.

First of all, how to dig.

The spade should go in vertically, or you'll not get the depth. A slight push forward before pulling back on it will bring the spitful out more easily. A spit is merely the term for the depth of the blade. I prefer to keep my top hand in pronation so that the soil can be turned off more easily, with less twisting of the wrist.

There is also on the market a patent spade which has something like bicycle handlebars on top of the shaft, spade at the bottom, and a back-thrust spur to give leverage. This is an excellent tool for the elderly.

There are three basic categories of digging.

The first, simplest and crudest, is sheer rough labour, slogging your way along the plot and leaving great lumps of earth lying turned up. These will, of course, need fining down later, but that is partly your intention. For if the plot is fairly clear of weed, and moderately well off in humus, you plan to leave those lumps to be well-chafed and broken by wind, rain and frost during the winter.

There is, however, one thing to beware about this. Don't dig your ground if it's too wet—if the soil clogs your boots. I did, one autumn, when I thought I had no choice. The rain and frosts, subsequently, didn't come and there were only hard winds which simply baked the clods hard. By next spring, which turned out as wet as the autumn had been, I had an even harder job of breaking down the soil. More sticky boots and more consolidated soil. In some places I gave up and crunched the top into a rough shingle and found, in the coming late summer, that I still had last year's spade marks under the surface. The potatoes had become misshapen by growing round and between the knobs of adobe, and some other crops didn't do very well at all because of it.

A refinement of digging is trenching and, in conscience, I must tell you about the third category, double-digging.

Trenching is easier, and almost defines itself.

Split your plot in half, lengthways. It's often convenient, and it's also psychologically more rewarding, to see apparently greater progress even if it is only along half of your land.

Dig a trench at one end, one spit deep. Lift the soil from the trench into a heap at one side. Break up the soil at the bottom of the trench, spread and chop in some manure on top of it, then dig another trench a foot behind the first, simply shifting the new soil into the vacant space. If it works out right, you reach the end with one empty trench, into which you tip the heap of soil from the first one. And then you start on the other half.

Double-digging is much more strenuous. Frankly, I gave up in a few minutes the only time I tried it, and you shouldn't *need* to do it either unless you're converting a long-established field. Otherwise it's for purists or masochists. If you're either, make your trench two feet wide and break up the soil on the bottom. Skim off the turf from the next trench you dig, lay it face down in the first, break it up, then add the soil. Start all over again.

Why are you digging so thoroughly, anyway? Essentially, to save yourself a lot of trouble later, by letting the weather take on the next stages of the work.

Plants need fine soil, but firm soil. If you dig rough, the air gets into the soil to nourish it, the water gets in and, with frost, helps to break it down and then drain away. With more hoeing and raking, in early spring, the soil should be a friable tilth, settling well, so that eventual young and delicate roots won't be damaged by movement as unprepared soil shifts. And this same period of digging is the best time for feeding the land.

Don't dig in the summer. You'll want to keep in as much moisture as possible and hoeing is all the ground should need—stirring the top inch so that air gets in and a sort of dust mulch is created which is a barrier to ground moisture reaching the surface and escaping by capillary action. And don't dig up the sub-soil; it will probably be heavy, very likely clay, and it's best left down there where it belongs, gradually turning into deeper top-soil under the action of manures and regular gardening.

You are only going to *want* to dig once a year, and once a year is also advised from the land's point of view. So you might as well feed the land at the same time.

If you're trenching, it's worth layering in good, well-rotted manure as you do it. Only certain root crops will object, as I shall show later, and even then not unless they meet it at once. If you're rough digging, scatter manure on the surface at the same time and it will find its way in, strengthening the soil, giving it moisture-retaining body, and releasing a lot of its needed nutrients. But no manure should go on to the plot unless it is well-rotted.

The easiest way of digging, according to some of my neighbours, is to put a machine on to the land. You can hire one, for several pounds plus your own petrol, and career around after it as it churns up the surface noisily. I have only used one, years ago, for cutting long, matted grass and it nearly killed me. It did kill, out of control, several roses of which I was fond. But another neighbour of mine, who had a man run a petrol-driven plough over his plot, was delighted at the even, fairly friable consistency of the soil after only about an hour. It was only later that he found, when planting, that the soil had been dug to about two inches. Some of his crops did not prosper. Next year, he has decided, he will be using his spade and as far as I am concerned—in the early years, at least—this can't be avoided.

But let me now outline Dr. Shewell-Cooper's other idea.

His conception—and he's practised it with success for years at his home at Arkley Manor in Hertfordshire, besides successfully writing and broadcasting about it—is of the no-digging garden. Organic gardening, in fact, and distinctly labour-saving it looks.

He advocates a mass of compost, well-rotted organic food, which he layers thickly on the ground, constantly replenishing it.

The worms come up for it and pull it down, perhaps for several feet. In doing so they tunnel (or dig) the soil and, more importantly, regenerate more nitrogen, phosphate and potash than they consume. In their busy life-cycle, they are building and distributing goodness throughout the soil. A few months after I'd fed and worked my chemically killed plot, the worms were back in their hundreds and the other living organisms by then also working for me must have been in their billions.

Even the surface compost, for as long as it stays there, is working, inhibiting weeds. Shewell-Cooper's practice is to pull out the few which show, leaving the compost to smother the rest, and to stop them seeding. Hoeing, without compost, which is the accepted way of keeping weeds down, will nevertheless chop off and allow to be implanted the thousands of weed seeds which can lie dormant for years until, on subsequent hoeing and digging, they come up, regerminate and grow again.

The drawback in your case, as a presumed beginner, is that Shewell-Cooper's system needs a great deal of compost. He has bays of it at Arkley, each bay in a different stage of decomposition. It needs time to build up that kind of reserve, and a great deal of raw material and space, and several years for it to take effect fully on the land. One year, soon, I'll give it a good try. If it saves me from digging, I shall be his follower and his system's anti-slave.

3 COMPOST

What of compost, then? What is it, and how do you get it?

Largely, you develop your own, although you can buy commercial composts in varying amounts and for varying purposes, and certainly the John Innes composts for seeding and potting are worth having for starting vegetables at home.

Very little organic material goes into my dustbin. Every scraping of kitchen waste goes into the plastic bags the council provides and eventually into the compost heap on the allotment.

Build it up in layers, keep it ventilated, occasionally watered, and warm. Introduce an activator from time to time—a proprietary brand, such as a sprinkling of garotta, or a slaking of lime and soil. That's the simple summary of compost-making but the process can be much more complex and satisfying, if you want.

A compost heap is a kind of oven, working at what would be a very low heat for the kitchen, but still generating anything from between 70 and 140 degrees Fahrenheit. At that top heat it is killing off a lot of harmful diseases and weed seeds. All it needs is a container, allowing air and water to get inside, and just about any kind of organic matter as the 'casserole' ingredients.

Build it on clean, cleared soil, with bricks laid on it to allow for ventilation below, and twigs between and above them to help drainage and containment. You can help the worms get to the compost by building a soil column in the middle, between the bricks. The sides should be of planking, nailed to strong corner posts, and with either gaps or holes for ventilation. The front panel should, of course, be easily removable.

Build up the layers of raw material about nine inches thick, with a thin inter-filling of garotta dust or lime and soil. About three to four feet is high enough, with a thin starter layer of manure or fertiliser on top. The whole should be covered with something permeable—say an old rug, which will keep the heap warm while letting the rain through to it.

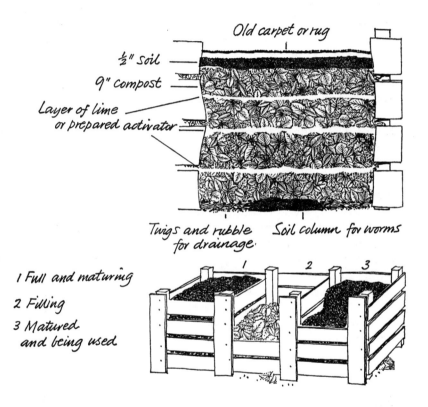

Old carpet or rug

½" soil

9" compost

Layer of lime or prepared activator

Twigs and rubble for drainage.

Soil column for worms

1 Full and maturing

2 Filling

3 Matured and being used

As the rubbish rots, and heat builds up, it develops a ferocious civil war of micro-organisms—bacteria gone berserk. At the peak of their feeding and internecine killing, the big battalions move up through the soil column. That is, the worms will come and eat them up. I'm a squeamish man, but there are fewer satisfactions, as a gardener, than seeing the long, finger-thick, bright magenta worms which grow and prosper in a successful compost heap, glistening against the almost charcoal colour of rotted vegetation. And it, and they, will then of course go on to the garden, to carry and spread richness through it.

Ideally, build three bays—one heap started, a three-month-old heap alongside, and one nearing readiness at six months beside that. The first 'casserole' to be cooked should last until the next one is ready, by which time you'll have started another successor.

If you want to know more about compost-making, there are two very good sources. You can buy a booklet from the Soil Association at Walnut Tree Manor, Haughley, near Stowmarket in Suffolk. And you can join Lawrence Hills' Henry Doubleday Research Association at Convent Lane, Bocking, near Braintree in Essex, which specialises in natural gardening.

There are proprietary compost containers for sale, but it's more fun and much cheaper to build your own.

There's also an American method—the black sheet method—which is simpler, because it does without bays, but it is untidier. It merely requires the layering of rubbish and activator, covered thinly with soil, and then with a thick black plastic sheet, held down by bricks. You take off the sheet to add the next layer once you've gathered enough material.

I use a version of both methods by keeping my rubbish in a black plastic dustbin bag until it's full enough to move up to the allotment. By then the material's well on the way to rotting—black, smelly and nasty, oozing with rich juice.

There are other ways of getting food for the land.

Most popular are local riding-stables. If you can find one with manure for sale, make sure it's well rotted before using it. On heavy soil, the dung should have a fair amount of straw mixed in it but it can be used, as it were, pure on light, sandy soils. Chicken manure is said to be even better, but it is chemically hot and should therefore be used sparingly. Probably the best source is a mushroom farm; having grown its mushrooms in an already rotted manure of horse-dung and peat, it then discards the manure. We found one farm which sold the stuff at twenty pence a bag, but we had to find the bags and transport.

Some municipal sewage farms now process a good, dried manure, at around fifty pence a large sack, and I have used this with success as a surface compost.

Grass cuttings make both a compost and a manure —fresh-laid at the bottom of a trench, say, for potatoes, rotted down in the heap as a top dressing. Don't put fresh cuttings on the surface; you'll keep in some moisture but you risk laying down grass seeds.

Don't worry too much about weeds. Get them out, whenever you can, either with the hoe or your fingers if they're close to tender plants, and if they're annual weeds leave them lying where they fall. The rows won't look the tidiest on the site but the weeds give some green mulch, helping to preserve moisture, and they'll gradually rot down for eventual digging in.

There is one wistful postscript to this chapter which one day I hope to adopt on some larger plot. Ideally, were my allotment large enough, fenced and secure, and the council indulgent, I'd like to see what a couple of pigs might do for it.

In theory, if I gave them a small, fenced area at a time, they'd dig it and manure it for me at the same time. They'd fatten a little while living off it, and a little more off kitchen refuse, even though that deprives me of some of my compost. And then I'd kill them and eat them, or at least sell them as fatteners. All I'd then need to do would be to hoe and rake and start planting.

Well, that's the theory anyway, but I suppose it would interfere with the careful planning and orderly progress of the plot. Pity, though.

4 TOOLS

But we're not on to the planting and growing, yet. We're still on preparation. It's worth considering, briefly, some of the tools you might find useful though not necessarily essential. The BBC's Pebble Mill programme instituted with brilliant success a series (and a book) called 'Dig This'. The programmes were based on a micro-allotment cultivation of which was by spade only. The transfer of a facsimile of the plot to the 1975 Chelsea Show was one of the show's hits.

You will be urged, however, to buy a whole battery of tools, the equivalent of a full set for golf. But a lot of rabbit golfers get round happily with a wood and five irons, so why shouldn't you manage in the same way on the land?

Besides a **spade**, what else do you need? A **fork**, yes, although you might use it infrequently. One fork will do; it's not necessary to buy another, with broad prongs, just to lift potatoes. Do it carefully, instead.

A **Dutch hoe** is essential, for weeding and breaking up the soil. A lot of people use it incorrectly, stabbing with it . It can indeed be used to break down rough-dug soil into a fair tilth, by pushing it steadily down at the edges of the ground, but it should properly be used as a sub-surface tool. Keep the edge sharp and slide it half an inch or so under the ground, keeping the blade horizontal, and chopping off the weeds as you meet them. The accompanying stirring of the soil lets in warmth and air and keeps in the moisture. A **draw hoe** is less necessary, although useful for making seed drills and for some weeding.

A **rake** is also necessary and—for refinement—a **sieve**.

A **five-pronged cultivator** I have found enormously useful for breaking down the top two or three inches of soil after rough digging, using it mostly with a pulling action but sometimes pushing too. Often it's not heavy enough for the conditions but works well enough, then, with a weight hung from the bottom of the shaft. The three-pronged cultivator, in some people's opinion, is even better.

Trowel and **hand-fork** are accepted as essential, mostly for transplanting, and a trowel, especially if it is narrow, can be less damaging to young roots than a **dibber.** I can't see the sense in buying a dibber when you can make one from a broken spade or fork handle, which is usually thick enough, but the D-shaped grip is better for complete control if the dibber is being used to firm in roots.

Now, what else are you going to need? Well, not everything, and not all at once. But eventually, and usefully, and in no particular order of preference, from the frivolous to the serious, the following——

A long, loose **pullover** which comes down to your buttocks and doesn't bare your kidneys to cold winds when bending. I use a sailcloth fisherman's smock, which keeps the wind out more effectively than wool.

Hard soled ankle boots.

Waterproof, rubber boots. Although it's sound advice not to tread down the soil if it's wet enough to stick to the boots, you can't always ignore the allotment in long periods of heavy rain. But at least, in this event, try to work from a piece of planking, and while you're at it, you might as well paint six-inch markers on one edge of the plank to ensure even spacing when planting.

A **wheelbarrow.** Usually, there's at least one on site. If so, fine. If not, padlock your own to something solid; there is not much honour among gardeners.

A **long hosepipe.** Most sites have standpipes with taps, but they are usually occupied all day by the man who, illegally, is running four plots at once, as an effectively subsidised market garden, for profit.

A **screwdriver.** To unfasten his hosepipe so that you can use yours.

A **watering can.** Essential.

A **variety of roses** for your watering can, from large bore to fine. If you can find a really fine rose for seed beds, which fits the average two-gallon polyurethane can, please let me know.

In passing, beware of how you use water. A sprinkling can be worse than nothing, when plants might need a real soaking, and you can wash away seed by watering without a rose, unless you wrap a piece of cloth round the end of the spout. If you have tanks with the standpipes, it's better to use water from them, which will have been warmed up during the day.

A **short-handled sickle**. I am right-handed and find I get the best angle and level of cut by resting my left hand, elbow-bent, on my right knee, with the right leg presented well forward. Take it slowly and steadily and don't try backhand table-tennis shots unless you want to put your wrist out.

String. And a **knife**. And **secateurs**.

Sticks, canes and poles. You'll discover when you need them and, if you ask, where to get them. Your local garden society is almost certain to be cheaper than anywhere else, unless you can steal safely from a wood.

Cold frames. Not always essential, but very useful. Cheaply made from old windows laid on a slope over bricks or timber. One at least, for bringing on young plants. Another, for amusement, to discover how hard it is to grow melons.

Cloches. These are, essentially, transparent tents for warmth and protection. Marvellous for bringing on early season vegetables, or helping tardy ones to catch up. Some people use plastic sheeting tied to upright sticks in a kind of corridor. Others use plastic-sheet tunnels but beware, then, of the soil drying out too much, or of creating a Farnborough wind-effect which harms any plants that aren't aerodynamic. Rich gardeners use glass, but you can, if you're lucky, buy sheets of this relatively cheaply from commercial greenhouses which occasionally go broke, or which are moved by councils wanting to build houses. I bought one hundred of these, in 1975, for ten pence each. I also found, from a rarer and free source, fifty sheets of transparent perspex which, when drilled and fastened by plastic wire, served beautifully. For simple, inverted-V glass cloches, there are very effective and inexpensive rubber clips.

Three types of cloche

A **greenhouse.** If you have one, you won't need to be told why you need one; if you haven't, accept that the investment repays itself in a very few years. Go for the modern shape with slightly inward sloping sides and a wide pitched roof, which allows maximum sun. Even if you wince at the cost, glass is better than plastic because it's less susceptible to dimming by chemical change or obscuring by algae. The new alloy frames are virtually indestructible. Make sure there's ventilation from the bottom to the top. Save money and build your own staging inside, to your own needs. Erect it, if you have the space, where you can get the maximum sun. A lean-to on a sunny wall can be very effective, if you've limited space, because the wall, if it's solid, will bounce the heat back inside. Even more effective is if you attach the greenhouse to a wall through which runs a central heating boiler flue, or which carries a fireplace chimney.

In your greenhouse, you can develop seedlings, or cuttings, or you can nurture young plants before bringing them into frames or cloches for hardening and thence to the open plot. You can start off beans, or peas, or brassicas, at a time when the weather is wrong for them outside or when you still haven't got around to preparing the ground for them. You can even grow food which never emerges from the greenhouse until you want to eat it.

Without a greenhouse, you can at least germinate seeds and bring on young plants indoors. **Seedtrays**, laid with peat and seed compost, pricked with seeds, watered, covered in dark plastic sheeting and set on the boiler, or a radiator shelf, or in the airing cupboard, will give you seedlings in days. Space on kitchen shelves will give you more seedlings. An airing in a sheltered part of the garden (bring them in at night) will soon have them ready for transplanting. **Plenty of pots**, and **a bag of potting compost**, will give you more flexibility in that phase.

And finally, a **freezer**, for storing surplus vegetables quickly, safely, and with little loss of flavour or nourishment. The old days of salting down vegetables in big sweet jars or earthenware crocks are largely gone, as is a good deal of the home pickling industry. Perhaps it's sad. But who's got the time, nowadays, for that kind of labour, and who's got the space? And, with the cost of earthenware, who's got the crocks? This book is about saving money, to survive, and, as well, about saving time and effort.

So, at a general scan, that should be all you need and you don't actually need all of it.

But you still need seed.

5 SEEDS

There's not a lot to be said here. Inevitably, you'll find your own likes and dislikes, in your own time.

Three years ago, I was buying from three or four seedsmen. Now I'm down to Sutton's alone.

Their advice is as good as it is simple. 'Choose your vegetables carefully, taking care of all the family preferences, and then select the variety that will suit you best. Good seed catalogues take pains to describe the particular characteristics of each variety.'

And so they do. If you choose to buy seeds at random, going mostly by the picture on the packet, you'll not get nearly as much value from your plot as you will by planning properly.

Many seedsmen now, for example, rate their vegetables for freezing qualities as well as for taste, size, proliferance. An hour's careful study, before buying, balancing what you can get against what you might be prepared to give up, makes a great difference.

The same kind of paperwork should leave you with an allotment book. You should have a plan of the plot showing the rows of seeds together with details of their nature, planting time, cropping time. There should be room for your own findings on the crop which will help you decide on the same or different seeds next time. And from the plan, you will know what to rotate and where. It is better not to grow successive crops of the same family in the same place. Where there were beans before, for example, is where next you might plant cabbages.

There are three main groups of vegetables.

Peas and beans are in one, fixing nitrogen in the

soil and thriving on well-manured ground. Salad crops and potatoes come into this group.

Next are the roots—carrots, parsnips, beet—which must not be freshly manured.

Then come the brassicas—cabbages, sprouts, cauliflower—longer-growing and cropping, mostly, in the autumn and winter (filling the so-called 'green gap'). If you can, divide your plot into five sections; one each for these groups, one for oddments and fruit, tomatoes, courgettes say, and one for your compost heap and tool and stick storage. Suggested plans are dealt with later.

Back, briefly, to the seeds themselves. A lot you can bring along at home, until they're ready for planting out. But you can't transplant root crops, so don't try. Pelleted seeds (each seed coated in a dry but soluble material) are very effective, and because of their manageable size you can plant them exactly where you want them to grow, saving thinnings and making the cost of a packet go further. But because of the need for the coating to dissolve they will take longer to germinate and must be given plenty of water. Seeds will keep for years, in many cases, particularly in the foil packets you sometimes get, and even more so if you store them in some container and place where there is virtually no atmospheric change. Some vegetables, for example endives, are said to grow better from older seeds. But I have also found that using old pea and bean seeds I have had to sow them more thickly and water them more.

Onions can be grown from autumn-sown seed, although I prefer to plant sets in the spring or to plant shallots kept back from the previous year's crop. Broad beans can also go in during November, but again I prefer a spring sowing; I resent laying down winter food for the mice.

6 BEANS

The dominant feature of any allotment, from spring to autumn, is the colour green. It's what gardening is mostly about, and if a lot of it provides only compost in the end, a massive amount is for eating.

Supreme over all, to my thinking, are beans.

You can't grow too many of them, and there are many to choose from.

Of the **broad beans** we have tried, the variety we have now settled on exclusively is **Masterpiece Green Longpod**. Sutton's recommend their sowing between February and April but I have had reasonable pickings from planting them as late as June. They grow five to seven seeds in a pod, freeze well, look pretty and taste superb. Even heavier croppers are **Exhibition Longpod** and **Colossal**.

Because Masterpiece develop a plant standing some two feet, I prefer them about a foot apart giving them room. Smaller varieties can be as close as six inches apart, but this can cause extra difficulty in moving among them to hoe and pick, if you've planted a great many.

Plant a new row every fortnight, so that you get a succession of beans coming to perfection through the early to mid-summer. Masterpiece seems fairly resistant to the curse of the broad bean, black-fly, but you'll have to watch out for it. Once on the plant, the fly spreads fast and it could result in a badly damaged crop. A quick spray with an insecticide will curb it, if you get at it quickly and thoroughly, and you can help further by pinching out the tops of the plants once the white flowers are out. It's this sweet, three-inch growth which in part attracts the fly in the first place. The tops themselves, chopped raw, make a delicious addition to summer salads.

You can sow broad beans in the winter for an early spring crop, but they are then vulnerable to mice. They might survive if, before you plant them, you put the beans in a jar with a teaspoonful of paraffin, shaking them enough so that the stuff taints the surface of the seeds.

Once your crop is over—and this applies to all beans—don't pull the dead or dying plants out. Chop them off at ground level and throw them on the compost heap, but leave the roots in for they are fixing the nitrogen for successive crops.

Before your broad beans are finished, you should be picking **French beans—dwarf** or **climbing**.

Sow these from April to July, grow them about nine inches apart, and pick continuously while the pods are young, so that the plant will keep producing more. It's criminal to cut them; they should be eaten whole, smothered in butter. Blanched, they freeze well, as do broad beans.

In my experience, French beans are virtually trouble-free and the most work you should have with them is some weeding, some watering in dry spells, and pinching off the tops of bigger varieties to contain plant growth and increase pod growth. My only disappointment is that the purple-podded varieties turn green when they're boiled.

This prominent purple appearance, incidentally, makes a dwarf French bean—say, **Kinghorn Waxpod**—as pretty as any conventional garden flowers and for two months I'd rather see them in my front garden than flowers. Why don't more people grow more vegetables in their front gardens? Courgettes, sweetcorn, globe artichokes, and, of course, beans, are all attractive and decorative growths and they make a change from roses and dahlias, besides being much more productive.

Runner beans, in which I include climbing French beans, don't in general fit into a small town gardens unless you've got a sunny fence doing nothing but keeping neighbouring dogs out, or a garden-dividing frame which only supports sweet peas.

Architecturally, runner beans are a highly satisfying

crop, because with them you can release some of your frustrated building instincts. As with all of this family, you are going to need a well-dug, well-manured area, a readiness to weed constantly once the plants start climbing, and of course a structure for them to climb. On an allotment, and if your crop is good, you are going to get a fairly heavy and wind-catching mass, at about the time the late summer and early autumn winds are building up. So if you want to avoid the frequent sight of a row of bean poles lying flat, build well.

Of the bean frames, there are four popular styles.

The first is the ridge-tent shape, long rows of long poles leaning towards each other and lashed near the tops. They should be strengthened with cross-bars. Under this tall roof, incidentally, there's usually room for a planting of cabbages as well.

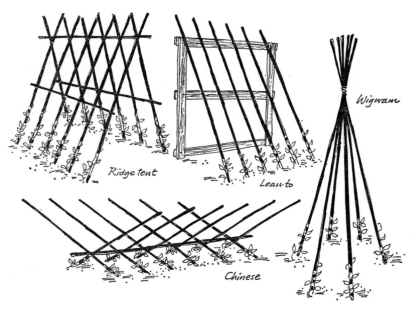

Permanent frames of heavy poles or iron piping are frequent. Generally, these carry a vertically hung netting, or support lean-to poles.

Permanent frames are not my choice. They deny the principle of rotation and there is a risk of root-rot spoiling the plants.

The wigwam shape is effective, giving room for six or seven plants in relatively little space, and with this system you can have clumps of beans in many different places.

I have also used, successfully, a style borrowed from the Chinese. The poles are crossed as in the ridge tent but are lashed together only a foot or two above the ground. The full run of pole projects outward at an easier climbing angle, the plants shade each other less from the sun, and the hanging beans are easier to see and pick.

Some people recommend long-lasting aluminium poles, expensive to buy but rarely needing replacement. It's been argued, however, that in hot weather these can become too hot for the runners.

Sowing is best delayed until the middle of May, unless you've been bringing on young plants in the greenhouse or under cloches. The seeds should go into soft soil, pressed in by thumb, a few inches away from the pole and underneath its rise. Poles should be a foot apart. I prefer working two bean seeds into each spot. The weaker can be nipped off or, if it looks like a warm and moist summer ahead, both can be given their chances on the same pole.

Some of the beans now in the catalogue are bred to grow pods well over a foot long. Find out first. Otherwise, if you leave ordinary beans to that length, you're going to get a hard and stringy vegetable. Pick them young and frequently except where you want to grow some for next year's planting, in which case, let the pods ripen completely before taking them off.

Once the plants are established, give them a good mulching (straw, manure or peat) to keep the moisture in. Pinch off the tops once these reach the top of the poles. And water them.

In the freak summer of 1975 mine survived the unexpected frost in June, but sagged under the hot, dry weeks that followed. The flowers didn't set and the pods didn't come, not in any number anyway, simply because I neglected to water them. I cut them down in frustration, in September, only to find that the warm moist weather which then came produced an entirely new flowering and cropping on those beans with which my more patient neighbours had had similar problems.

My preference with climbers nowadays is more for the French than the runner, again eaten whole, if they're picked young and not too long. The **purple-podded** variety is magnificent. Among the runners, **Enorma** *is* enormous. **Prizewinner**, **Achievement**, and the white-seeded **White Achievement** are popular.

In the last year or two, a new bean has been developed, the **Fiskeby.** It's described as enormously rich in protein, a sort of wonder bean. I had no success with it when it first came out, but that's probably my fault. Thompson and Morgan have developed it and, if you've room and time, it might be worth your trying.

7 PEAS, SALADS, ONIONS AND ROOTS

As I claim for beans, so is it claimed for **peas**—you can't have too many.

As with broad beans, I am now down to one variety, **Miracle**, a two-foot plant, heavy cropping, with long, dark-green pods of about ten peas, sweet and good for freezing. They seem durable in varied weather conditions, although they do need strong supporting.

Peas, too, should be sown in sequence, in some cases from as early as Christmas-time (for a spring crop) otherwise from February–March until the summer. Don't put them in a V-shaped drill. Take out a flat-bottomed, shallow drill, about six to nine inches wide, and march the seeds along it in three rows, a few inches apart. Drills should be about two feet apart, or you could find it hard to get between them for weeding and picking.

They need plenty of water, when sown, to bring on germination. In a dry period, and this can apply to most plants, it can be useful to give them a special kind of watering. That is, keep the soil from the shallow trench carefully away from water and soak the trench very thoroughly, without letting water get up the sides of it or along its edges. Plant the seeds and then put the removed soil back, carefully, and without watering on top of it. The dry, loose, soil stops all that moisture escaping by capillary action to evaporate, and keeps it where it's needed, helping germination. But after a few days, you must water normally, and carry on doing so.

When the peas are a few inches high, earth the soil up around them, gently but firmly, to protect them against wind and to keep in the moisture. Hazel twigs are the best for support and these, too, should be pushed towards each other at the tops, against the wind. Trim any long sticks and use the bits as ground-level fill-in for extra shelter and early support. An early hoeing will keep the weeds down and a mulch between the rows will help with moisture.

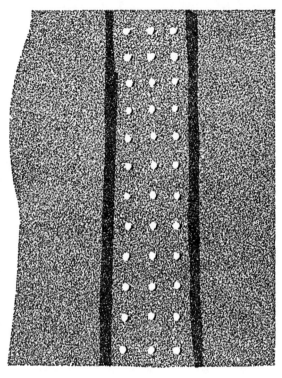

Peas planted in a foot-wide drill an inch deep in three rows about 3" apart

You can make better use of space with peas and with runner beans by ladder planting. Essentially, this means a north–south row of runner beans and one of peas as the 'poles' of the ladder, and fairly close east-west rows of salad crops between them, as 'rungs'. They're mutually helpful over shelter and moisture conservation.

Although you'll find your own preferred varieties of peas from a good catalogue, it's worth remembering there are many types. These include tiny French peas, purple-podded, marrow-fat and the splendid **'mangetout'**, producing

37

pale-green, flat, fleshy pods with small seeds inside, which are boiled and eaten whole, hot or cold.

The accepted summer salad is **lettuce**—over-rated, I think, except for the crisp **Cos** and **Webb** varieties. Lettuce, too, prospers best on previously manured ground, raked to a fine texture. You can start sowing in late October, under cloches, transplanting to other cloches from the New Year onwards and into the open ground as the weather warms. Sow as late as August for an autumn crop. Find out from your catalogues which varieties will respond for which season.

If lettuce is planted directly into the open, sowing should be in shallow drills about six inches apart. As, inevitably, you will have to do a lot of thinning and some transplanting, you can help by thinning as you sow. I mix our seed with fine sand or granular compost and sometimes with radish or beet-root, shaking it out carefully and sparingly.

Radish, maturing quickly, will leave gaps in the lettuce as it's picked; it makes thinning easier. Early lettuce, as it comes out, makes more room for the later beetroot. There's no need to throw away lettuce thinnings; they can go straight into sandwiches with other things.

You will, of course, grow too much and pick too little, and it will crowd up or bolt away or go slimy. Don't worry. The seed is cheap and the plant makes good compost.

If you want summer salads, there are other things to grow. Excess **cabbage**, picked young and chopped raw. **Brussel sprout** and **broad bean** tops and, indeed, young **sprouts** which taste nutty. **Endives**, **chicory** and **sorrel**. Watch out for sorrel; all you have to do is plant it, leave it and pick up. It has a crisp, lemony tang in a salad. But it's also regarded as a weed and will grow and spread like one if you don't control it.

Endives are hard to grow, being temperamental. They're at their best on a raised bed of light soil, with plenty of water and no fertiliser. You'll have to blanch them by covering with a pot or a piece of wood or slate before picking. **French chicory**, Sugar Loaf for example, sown in June and July will prolong the salad season. Buy **watercress** from the

38

greengrocer, unless you've got a clean stream nearby where it grows wild, and leave **mustard and cress** to your children, unless you want to grow a carpet of it as a mulch.

Radishes are a long-lasting, and indeed, recurring delight in the summer and are among the easiest of crops. If the ground is fine, you can start sowing, thinly and shallowly, from March until early autumn, every two or three weeks.

Just leave them and watch them grow, except that in long dry spells they'll need watering. It's said that they shouldn't be planted in summer, because they turn hot and dry, but I like radishes that way too. I split my selections between **Cherry Belle** and **Scarlet Globe** (round and fat) and the longer, red-and-white **French Breakfast**. Eat them chilled from the fridge, with a smear of butter on each.

I haven't grown **celery**, but if and when I do it's not going to be the performance some people make of it. Trenching and manuring, transplanting from seed boxes, watering, tying the leaves, earthing up (twice), and further blanching with cardboard tubes—it all sounds like a lot of work. I shall buy self-blanching celery which, although liking manure, doesn't need trenches, doesn't need earthing or much other attention. It's not as hardy as the other kind, but it's simpler and quicker.

Another useful salad is the **spring onion**, which is sown mixed with radish seed for the same thinning out effect. Again, this is a crop which can be left to look after itself, and if you don't pick it all in time for salad uses, it's good as a late, more swollen, onion for cooking.

Onions themselves (in which I include shallots) are much easier to grow than most literature about them will suggest.

Ideally, the ground should have been deeply dug, during the winter, with manure worked in, and left to weather. By February or March, it should have been broken down, raked fine and then, when dry, trodden firm. However, I did magnificently with onions as the first crop on my previously sterile plot, with very little cultivation of the ground and no manure or compost at all.

If you *have* prepared the ground in this way however and are growing from seed sown in trays the previous January, the seedlings go into the ground in March–April, about nine inches apart. Onion sets go in a month later, and there should be one foot between rows.

Push the bulb gently but firmly into the surface, leaving the top half showing. After a week or two, when the first green shoot is through, you may have to work round the rows again, re-seating those which the roots or the worms have pushed loose. You can guard against this, to some extent, by indenting the ground with your thumb before planting. I started my onions going very comfortably, one year, by settling them into little pockets of old silver-sand from the children's previous year's sand-pit. Some gardeners advocate drawing shallow drills, placing the sets, and then topping up with soil, but I've never lost more than seven or eight sets in a hundred by my method. Altogether, I find sets preferable, as labour-saving and easy-growing, but onions grown from winter seeds tend to be bigger.

They will need hoeing regularly, and some finger-weeding in case the hoe cuts the bulbs or disturbs their fairly precarious early seating. By mid-summer, you might see some of the leaves forming a phallic-shaped tip. Unless you want the onion to go to seed (and I doubt you do) pinch off these leaves as low as possible.

By mid-August into September, you may judge the onions are about right for size, and showing signs of ripening. Leaves will be yellowing faintly, for instance, and bending. It's now that you bend them over properly, an inch or two over the bulb, but without disturbing the roots. They'll mature well from now, and be ready for lifting within a fortnight or so. If the weather is dry and sunny, lay them out to ripen—otherwise, finish them off inside. They'll store, in a shed, either in ropes or bunches (if you've the time or ability to plait them) or on slatted trays. A ten-rod plot should see you through the winter with onions.

Shallots effectively get the same treatment, but a bit more space, for one shallot can develop a dozen more. They should have grown enough by mid-July for finishing off. The easiest way to tell is if they are then lying almost flush with the surface; they come loose at a very light touch. Lift them and lay them down to ripen. Cook with them, pickle them, and keep enough back for another sowing in the following March. Three or four thirty-foot rows will give you masses.

The onion's close relative, the **chive** is probably better grown at home in any small space available. You won't want many, and they should be handy for the kitchen. But **garlic** is worth growing on the allotment. Plant separate cloves, an inch deep, in March, and watch them come up. They're never as fresh or as cheap in the shops as from the allotment, and they store well in ropes.

Onions have one particular enemy (apart from too wet a summer) and that's the onion-fly. If it gets your plants, you've no choice but to get them out and burn them. There are chemicals you can apply, when sowing, to ward off the fly and lesser pests. But there is also a simple, natural, precaution. The onion-fly is not greatly fond of the carrot-fly, and it's mutual.

Make them into potentially bad neighbours and, most probably, the pests will avoid both vegetables. Two rows of onions followed by two rows of carrots have kept both pests away from my allotments.

As with onions, you can leave the ground fairly rough for **carrots** until they're ready for sowing—which is in March and April for the early varieties for picking in June and July, and until mid-July for the autumn and early winter crops. But they should be sown—in half-inch drills, a foot from each row—in a fine tilth and the ground (as with parsnips) should be clear of fresh manure which would fork the roots if they met it. If you have a good depth of soil you can grow long varieties, which are better for storage. In more shallow soil, the short, stumpy kind with a cylindrical growth rather than a tapering growth, are fine. This kind is good for early season catch-crops.

Thin the carrots as soon as you can, and don't do it when the sun is shining. The best time is on a dull evening, or with rain threatening. If it's not going to rain, water the rows thoroughly after thinning, and throw the discards on to your compost heap well away from the survivors. Carrot tops bruise when they're handled, 'bleeding' a juice which, if left behind, does attract the carrot-fly.

Those you don't eat immediately can be stored easily in boxes of dry sand. Young carrots, blanched, cooled and with their skins rubbed, freeze well; so do older ones, peeled, sliced and blanched. Yet more can be left in the ground surprisingly late in the year until they're needed, but you would need to lay straw over them in sharp, frosty weather.

Young, small **parsnips**—trimmed, peeled and blanched—also freeze well, but they're better fresh and these, too, can stay in the ground a long time. If they're still there in March, however, it's time you got them out and stored them as with carrots, or they'll start again, for it's in March that you should be sowing new ones, through until May. Put them in shallow drills, rows a foot apart, and each root (pelleted seeds, again, save thinning) about nine inches from the next.

Beetroot are worth giving space to. It's a pity their qualities in salads cause them to be overlooked as hot vegetables, or in bortsch. They freeze well, sliced or whole after a good half-hour's boiling, and they pickle well. And they grow almost more easily than anything else. I prefer the **Boltardy**, which don't bolt. Plant them in two-inch drills, about nine inches apart and in rows one foot apart. Leave them until you need them, up to the end of the year if necessary, but be ready to cover them against frosts.

Beetroot—like seakale and asparagus—were once maritime plants and when they're showing reasonably you'll help their growth by giving them a salt watering. About one teaspoon to a two-gallon can should do each row, but don't repeat the dose.

A good beetroot needs about four inches on each side to fatten in comfort, but even with pellet seeds you'll often get two or three growing side by side. I've usually found I can wait until they're as big as a lemon before thinning them to singles, and in this way I've got a good size for pickling. Besides Boltardy and **Globe**, Sutton's also have a golden beet which doesn't bleed and whose tops can be cooked as spinach. Another newish variety is **Snowwhite** which is, indeed, white and therefore non-staining. It also only needs half the usual cooking time.

I refuse to say anything of **spinach** itself, because I loath it, but they tell me it's easy to grow, for summer and winter.

Other roots worth growing are **turnips** and **garden swedes**, if only because, when mashed in with carrots, they're superb, and because small, golf-ball-sized turnips, boiled and glazed with honey, are even more superb. Also young turnip tops make very tasty greens.

Turnips can be sown (not too closely, or they'll bolt) from April to early July, and swedes preferably in June. Both need early thinning until they're about six inches apart, except for those you are growing for tops. They should go in during August or September and should not be thinned. Regular watering should keep them healthy. You can store them like carrots. Freeze turnips when they're young and swedes in purée form.

Once the plants are any size at all, I'd recommend handling them with gloves unless you want badly scratched hands.

Two less usual root crops, which my wife is trying out this year, are **celeriac** and **white salsify.** The former gives big, round roots rather like swedes, the other longer, thinner roots, rather like leek stems. Celeriac does taste like turnip, and salsify has a delicate taste hard to describe. Perhaps it's a bit like artichoke. It is sometimes called the vegetable oyster.

8 POTATOES AND BRASSICAS

The vegetable I have doubts about is the **potato.** There's a lot of hard work, and a lot of mystique, for a crop that takes up space, hangs around a long time, is sometimes uncertain, subject to various ailments and has diminished in variety under Common Market regulations but as their supply and price are so unpredictable in the shops they're worth while on an allotment.

In my own case, I grow them indifferently, because, not caring about them greatly, I grow them carelessly. But many people do seem to enjoy working them and do well out of it, so here goes.

There are usually three crops—early, second early and maincrop—self-explanatory in that that's when they come during the spring–autumn period. There is one generally accepted way of growing potatoes, plus a variant that seems much simpler and which I'll describe later.

In any case, you'll need to begin with seed. These should be potatoes about the size of a golf-ball; larger ones can be cut in half. Lay them preferably in wooden trays, in a light and not too cold place, to sprout. When several shoots are about the length of a fingernail rub off all but the three strongest-looking, or at least those three strong ones which are reasonably apart from each other. All the shoots you keep should be pointing in the same direction and should point upwards when the seed is planted.

Planting takes place in March, April or May, depending on which seasonal crop you've bought, so you should have picked out the seeds and laid them for sprouting some three or four weeks earlier. Incidentally, the farther north they come from the less they have probably been affected by bugs the previous year, which is presumably why the Scottish varieties are popular.

The accepted practice now is to dig a trench about a foot wide and a spit deep and manure it. One school says don't use fresh manure and that if you've nothing else a fertiliser of phosphate of lime, sulphate of potash and sulphate of ammonia should do. Another school says fresh manure is fine, or a thick bed of fresh grass cuttings, and that the seeds can

be popped on to it, at about one foot intervals. They're then covered with the fine soil that's come from the trench, and another trench begun two to three feet away. Wood ash, or leaf mould, can be added to the soil for its softness helps protect against surface scars forming on the potatoes.

As the young leaves begin to appear at the surface, you should cover them with a ridge of soil, drawn up with a hoe from between the trenches. Keep on with this earthing up until the ridges are about a foot high. They should be in an inverted U, rather than an inverted V, so that the flattened top will let

46

water through to the tubers. If you don't earth up well, the potatoes will go green, and taste bitter; it's their natural response to light. There are plenty of ailments which can affect a potato, but at least earthing up will stop that, and plenty of humus will stop scab. Keep the ridges clear of weed, and a good watering with Bordeaux mixture (essentially, copper sulphate and quicklime) or Burgundy mixture (copper sulphate and washing soda) should guard against blight, once the leaves are through.

When the plants have flowered and are fading and drying that is the time to lift. Do it when the ground is dry. Make sure that the potatoes are dry when you store them and that any which you might have damaged with the fork are kept separate for immediate kitchen use.

The choice for storage is a clamp on the allotment, or boxes, or a dark, frost-proof shed or cellar. You can, of course, leave them in the ground until you need to use them, and if you're not growing many, and aiming in any case at the time when they're most expensive in the shops, this might be the best answer.

A clamp is tedious to make and still space-consuming. It involves clean, firm ground on which should be a layer of straw. The potatoes are then heaped on that, covered again with straw, and then with more earth, except for a straw ridge

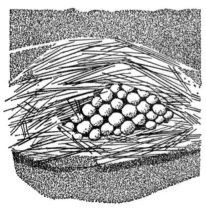

kept exposed for a few days to allow the potatoes to sweat. A couple of pieces of drainpipe are worked into the ridge for ventilation and these are then covered with straw caps. The clamp is then sealed and a ditch dug round it for drainage. When you want potatoes, you have to break into it and rebuild a section once again. Boring. As an alternative, they can be stored in sacks or in boxes containing dry sand, but they must be kept dark and warm against winter frost.

There's no choice about storage but there is, at least, about growing.

The man next to me—having, in any case, given his potato patch a good manuring and digging much earlier—simply built up his ridges before planting, using a well-sieved topsoil. He then ran his dibber along the top, punching a six-inch-deep hole every foot. Into each hole went a half-handful of soft compost, then a tuber, then the other half-handful, and finally whatever topsoil was needed to fill up the hole. He got thirty pounds to a row, and barely had to touch them except for a little hand-weeding.

One advantage of this system is that you can better carry out the tip experts urge with potatoes—of growing catch-crops between the rows. That is, early lettuce, or radish, or carrots. It's hard to do this when you're earthing up from between the rows, where the catch crops would lie. Next season, I shall grow half of my potatoes in this way and the rest conventionally, and see which works best.

There's another fallacy about potatoes. You will probably be told they'll dig your land for you. They don't. You do. Certainly if the soil is friable to begin with, they'll keep it so as the stems spread through it, and earthing and lifting will be the equivalent of a good forking over. But put potatoes into rough-dug soil and you'll get rough-shaped tubers, and not many of them either, for the energy of the stems will go into fighting their way out of this knobbly labyrinth.

A useful addition to the crop, useful for the kitchen and also for seeing whether you might like other varieties, is to grow potatoes at home, in large pots. Start them in a pot

48

half-full of soil and compost and when the leaves show, fill the pot up. There'll be enough for a meal in each pot.

I make no particular attempt to recommend varieties, as so many are not now available and you'll probably have to take what you're offered anyway. We continue to be unable to get **Pink Fir Apple** salad potatoes, but did enjoy the **Pink Desiree** maincrop last season. **Majestic** seem to do well and are popular, as are **Eclipse, Epicure** and the **Arrans.**

I have a similar mistrust of **brassicas** but partly, perhaps, because I haven't succeeded very well with them, and partly because I'd rather eat beans than cabbage. Mine often get eaten by mice, rabbits, pigeons and insects rather than me. The leaves are skeletal, the cauliflower hearts and broccoli spears premature and stunted, and half of my sprouts bolt wildly. I suspect it's basically because they sense I find them boring, and won't put out for me, where all around my neighbours have monstrous cabbage patches, guarded, netted and chemically cured. It's mostly the successful experience of my neighbours which follows.

Begin with a fine-tilth seedbed, which has had manure dug into it earlier, and which you'll keep in good shape with compost, fertilisers, pest-killers, hoeing and watering. And get your neighbours to prepare similar beds. With brassicas, you're better off in a co-operative with each gardener producing seedlings of one kind and swopping with others when the time comes for replanting.

Sprouting broccoli is usually ready at two seasons—some varieties between September and November (say, **Autumn Spear**) and others between February and April. They can be sown in one-inch drills in well-composted soil, in the bed or in a cold frame, and are transplanted about three feet apart when they're about four weeks old. Firm them in well, or the heads will be disappointing. Pick regularly, stop them going to seed, and they should last several seasons.

Firm-headed broccoli take a year to grow, so plan early. Their season is from about November to June, depending on the varieties chosen.

Brussel sprouts should crop between October and March, filling the green gap and, incidentally, freezing well. They are sown in March and April, firmly transplanted in May and June two to three feet apart, and hoed and watered well. When the lower leaves start to yellow, pick them off. And pick the buttons, which should be tightly packed around the stem, from the bottom up when they're ready. When the buttons are gone, sprout tops can be cooked like cabbages.

Cabbage generally does well in most soils, grows easily and is very hardy. They are sown in late spring for transplanting in July (eighteen inches apart, two feet from the next row) and should be edible in autumn and winter. Or sow in July and plant out in September for spring eating. Or sow in April and move in June, for summer eating.

They'll thrive better on ground manured for the previous crop—for example, on the patch in which you've left your undisturbed bean roots—and with hoeing and feeding.

Cauliflowers also like land in good fettle, well-manured and deeply dug. Sow under glass in January, transplanting from March and picking in the summer, or in the open in March and April, transplanting after two months and picking in late summer and early autumn. They need room—between two and three feet all round. What you and I have always called the hearts, real gardeners call 'curds' and some cooks call 'florets'. The main thing is, once they look right, start eating them. They can run to seed quite quickly in hot weather and it pays to shelter them on hot days by covering the hearts with a bent-over leaf.

It's not worth freezing cabbage—it can always be with you, anyway. Cauliflower and broccoli hearts freeze well, sprouts magnificently, but in any case you're not likely to have enough for freezing. They all take so much space you can only afford so many, and these you're likely to use fresh as they become ready.

9 COURGETTES AND ARTICHOKES

Another vast and roomy plant is the **courgette**.

This has still not caught on enough, although the older generation has always grown it as marrow. A marrow is only an overgrown courgette, and fairly tasteless unless used as a case for other things, or mixed into a ratatouille. The plant I mean gives out two or three five-inch-long vegetables every two or three days in the high summer and there's no better use for it than to fry it in garlic butter.

But do pick regularly. Five inches is long enough for a courgette and beware of leaving them. Last year I left one of three inches, went away for twelve days, and came back to find it two feet long and weighing over nine pounds.

The plants themselves last for weeks and are virtually indestructible, even after you think they're dying. But they do need room, for they can spread to a radius of two feet as well as growing nearly as high upwards.

The hardest part about them is starting them off and planting them out. We use a seed tray for the former, a cloche for the first two or three weeks in the open, a little compost and a lot of watering. The more water they get in dry weather the better, and especially if you plant them where they seem to do best, on a ridge or mound with a lot of manure and compost in it. You can cover your bet against their dying in this first fortnight by planting three seedlings together and chucking out the two eventual weaklings.

Apart from watering and picking, you can practically leave them alone. They'll keep the weeds down and they're very decorative in the garden. But you might need to approach the big ones with gloves.

Even more decorative are **globe artichokes** and

these will certainly go into our flower garden now. It's a pity to grow them on an allotment, anyway, because they are slow developing, space consuming, and susceptible to slugs. But they make handsome plants, several feet high, and eventually bear the strange thistle-like fruit so delicate in vinaigrette. The first we grew, we didn't even eat. The thistle was so pretty it just sat around as an ornament for some weeks as the bright-purple, honey-scented, shaving-brush hairs grew out of its top. Globe artichokes are, in any case, so prolific just across the channel that they are often in glut on the French market. It seems a great pity that some enterprising wholesaler doesn't ship them over from Brittany at a much cheaper price.

Jerusalem artichokes grow almost as a weed on one part of my allotment, but they are confined to a bank near a path. I ignore them until the autumn when the flowers have gone and the four-foot stems begin to yellow and wilt. That's when I root them up, although always missing enough so that a new crop appears the next year. That's when we drink that delicious cream of artichoke soup.

10 LEEKS, TOMATOES AND SWEETCORN

We might also get a fair amount of leek soup but for our preference for the **leek** as a rather lazily-grown fresh vegetable.

Although the kind we invariably buy is **Musselburgh**, the great leek centre of Britain is not Edinburgh but Newcastle and the surrounding areas of Northumberland and County Durham. But it is not the great, secretly-bred, jealously nurtured prize-winning monsters of that region that we grow; indeed, nowhere in this book is any consideration given to growing for exhibition rather than for simple eating. We grow small leeks, because we're lazy, but also because we prefer them small, slim, very juicy and succulent.

We sow them in March or April, in a fine tilth, and each year we say we'll do what everyone else does—transplant them in the summer into eight-inch dibber-made holes, well watered and composted, subsequently blanching them either with earth or little cardboard coats, until they're big and whitened and respectable. Anyway, that's what you *can* do; we never get round to it and we like them the way they taste.

Don't worry about leeks. They're very hardy, seem unaffected by pests and diseases, and can stay in the ground as long as necessary. But if you are growing big ones, they can have an extensive root spread, so give them at least a foot around when transplanting. And big ones will stand up better against the wind if, when blanching them, you use the cores of kitchen rolls, anchoring them with a stem of wire inside. (See page 54.)

An even stronger combination of preferred taste and laziness affects our attitude to **tomatoes**. There's almost as much mystique about these as about potatoes, and on my allotment it's unnecessary.

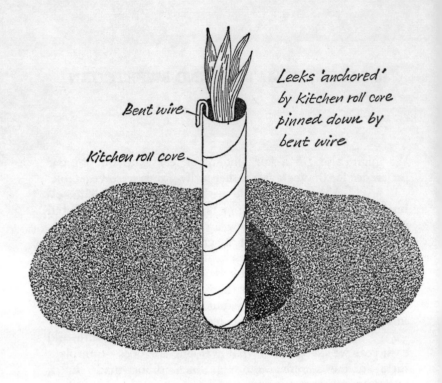

Leeks 'anchored'
by kitchen roll core
pinned down by
bent wire

Bent wire

Kitchen roll core

Now you can—if you have one—bring on trays of seedlings in your greenhouse; indeed, leave them there to grow into full, fruiting plants. You can move the seedlings from tray to a pot, and then 'pot them on', as they say, into a bigger pot, from time to time feeding them with proprietary medicines, or essence of soot, or animal dung. You will be growing them in seeding compost, then potting compost, perhaps with bonemeal or wood ash added. You will water them copiously, stake and tie them, confine the growth to one stem per plant, assiduously picking off any side shoots which develop, and picking off the tops once the plants meet from either side of the greenhouse under its ridge. You can mulch them, protect the green fruits from the dirty ground (and the birds and other nuisances) with sticks, or glass, or slate, and beat off the blight with liquid copper sprays. In short, make a constant and attentive veneration of them. Outside, you will want them under cloches or in cold frames during their early life, and you will worry about sudden frosts. And you will never be short of expert advice—and shared worry—from all the other gardeners growing them in the same way. But not from me.

Our tomatoes are free-thinkers and easy-growers. About the only thing they share in common with the rest is that they are moisture loving.

We buy the outdoor bush variety and, nowadays, exclusively the **French Marmande**.

This is the big, oddly shaped, sprawling kind, knobbly and creased, sometimes spheroid, rarely globular. There's not much seed in it, but a lot of firm flesh on it, and it is a good, rich, deep-red colour when it's fully ripe. It's specifically not recommended for glass. Try it and be converted; it is, you will discover, the tomato you mostly get in France as a salad.

Start it, as we do, in seed trays on the boiler at the end of March. Put the trays outside two or three weeks later, if the weather's not sharp, to harden. Three or four weeks later, transplant the biggest seedlings. If you don't have much well-dug rich loam available, make pockets of peat and compost in rougher soil. Soak them well, firm in the plants, dress the surface with a handful of top soil, and then virtually leave them alone. Water them regularly, though—tomatoes can take as much as two gallons a day every day in dry periods. A stone-filled pot or pipe buried alongside the tomato can take a lot of that water straight down to the roots.

By August, you should have monstrous plants, spreading like courgettes over several square feet of ground and in several directions, for I certainly don't pinch off side-shoots. Don't stake them, or pinch them short. Put sticks under the fruit, if you will, to lift them from the ground. I use perspex cloche sheets. If you can't be bothered, don't bother; they won't come to much harm. But it is probably worth netting them, loosely, against birds once they start to colour. We get well over a dozen fruit to each stem, and if that doesn't sound many, each one averages at about half a pound and some go up to twelve ounces.

They ripen well, but you can finish them off indoors either individually wrapped in something porous and stowed away somewhere warm or, as we prefer, simply by lifting the entire plant and hanging it up somewhere. If there are some ripening fruit on it, the gas they naturally give off circulates around the others, ripening them up as well. I then have a giddy month or two of peppered tomato sandwiches, and the heavy surplus joins the courgette crop in frozen ratatouille.

Some other good outdoor varieties are **French Cross** and **Sleaford Abundance**, and a colleague has had great success with the smaller, delicate yellow tomatoes, **Golden Queen**.

Like the Marmande variety and French beans, another continental crop I'd as soon see in the front garden is **sweetcorn**.

Start it in trays, like tomatoes. Plant out in manured ground in May or June, giving each plant about eighteen inches all round. If you plant rows, you'll probably see them fail. Sweetcorn is self pollinating, needing the wind instead of bees, so set it in blocks or boxes. Don't give it shade. As it grows to about four feet, it should find a lot of its own sunlight. When the cobs are grown they should feel tight and firm in your hand and the silky growth at the ends of the ears will be turning brown. Snap off the cobs and, to eat them at their best, eat them fresh. They can be frozen.

There's still a feeling about this foreign crop that it's exotic. Perhaps it is. But it's not hard to grow, and the only inhibition you should feel about it is the space it takes up. This and other factors—like time and effort—might deter you from trying other so-called exotics, such as aubergines, celeriac, kale, kohl rabi, salsify, melons and pumpkins.

Perhaps the objection to the luxury crop, asparagus, is well founded. I certainly wouldn't have the patience to give up space and time to a crop I couldn't harvest until its third year. But in other cases, why not? Try them, even if only in a small experimental section of the plot, for oddments. Get the main crops right first, of course, but after all that digging and weeding, you owe yourself some fun.

11 HERBS

Herbs, above all, are best grown near the kitchen door; it's inconvenient to have to go to the allotment just to pick up fresh seasoning. Claire Loewenfeld and Philippa Back have written a comprehensive guide, *Herbs for Health and Cookery*, which provides all the answers for the obsessive herbalist. As the authors point out, the Romans brought to Britain about 400 herb plants for culinary and medicinal use.

About a dozen are certainly worth growing in the garden, or in pots. For example:

Parsley (usually the curly kind). Needs rich, deep, shady soil but can cope with pots and window boxes and is best sown freshly each year.

Mint. Spearmint or the stronger **Bowles Mint** are the sauce herbs. Grow from cuttings or roots and preferably in pots, as the roots spread considerably.

Basil. Hard to grow, but it improves so many dishes. Needs warmth and feeding and does best, therefore, in pots where it can be brought indoors.

Bay. This can also be grown, for years, in a pot but it can also turn into a twenty-five-foot tree, which suggests eventual planting out. It likes shade and dislikes long frosts; otherwise it's hardy.

Rosemary. Another pot plant which will do very well in light, sheltered soil, growing tall if you let it. It doesn't like the winter.

Sage. Grows anywhere, but likes the sun. Split it, or take cuttings from it, to start it afresh every three years. Bees like it.

Thyme. Does better in the ground than in pots. It grows and spreads easily. Lemon thyme is also worthwhile.

Borage. We tried this one year, for chopping raw in salads, but sorrel is better and cucumber makes a better fruit cup. We also grew **rue**, poetically alongside rosemary, but it's a boring, vile-smelling plant and tea makes better tea. Tea is also better than **camomile**, but one day we shall grow a small lawn of that, for the smell it gives off when crushed under foot.

Garlic, of course, is essential, and is fine for the allotment. **Chives** are best grown in small quantity at home.

If you've space and inclination, others worth trying are **dill, summer savoury**, **sweet cicely** and **tarragon**.

You'll not actually *want* to grow dandelions—but if you've got them, the leaves make a good chopped addition to salad, as do young nettle leaves (boiling or drying takes out the poison). Other salad additives are nasturtium and celery leaves.

There is one other good home crop—**mushrooms**. They do well in sheltered odd spots around the garden, the spawn sown in compost free of soil, and indoors if there's good ventilation. Most seedsmen now sell mushroom spawn and many of them also sell container kits of prepared compost and spawn which produce regular crops over a couple of months or so. Afterwards, the compost is good garden mulch.

Besides all this, there is a practically limitless amount of food you can glean from the wild. Richard Mabey is the expert on that. Read his book *Food for Free*.

12 FRUIT

Down with privet.

It's a dreary, dusty, boring hedge that smells of cat's pee and it's also bad for horses. There are many better hedge materials and in my back garden two of the boundaries are made impregnable by blackberry bushes with some raspberry mixed in one side. There's another big **blackberry** clump on the allotment, and there's no finer, nor easier, fruit to grow.

If you're starting one off, give it a good, manured base. Thereafter, it looks after itself, only needing to have the thick, brittle-brown old wood cut out each October, once the berries have stopped. We get huge berries, fresh, for about three months, and enough spare for the freezer to last another six.

The only snag to a blackberry bush on an allotment is that it gets raided—by neighbours, if you're away for more than a week, and by birds. They're the greater problem, abetting the wind in casting seeds everywhere, so that there are sometimes scores of young brambles to be grubbed out every spring.

We also have labour-saving **strawberries.** In a year of normal weather, the most we have to do is pull out encroaching grass and net the patch against birds. Every three or four years, we transplant it, thinning at the same time. This is because we grow Alpines—the proper wild strawberries of the continent, the **Fraises du Bois.** They're small, about the size of a fingernail, which means you have to pick more for the weight of an average dishful, but they're very heavy croppers and very, very strong on taste and smell. The plants are about six inches apart and need neither trimming nor feeding. We

59

renew them by thinning—they don't send out suckers—and they also seem less vulnerable to birds than the bigger, more cultivated, varieties.

Of these, of course, there are some notable English kinds—particularly **Royal Sovereign, Redgauntlet**, and the **Cambridge Prizewinner** and **Rival**.

They don't have to be grown on the ground; they do well in those expensive earthenware strawberry barrels with holes in, or less expensive wooden ones, and I have seen them growing effectively from a punctured oil drum and a dustbin. There is also, now, a very successful system of growing them through holes in long, four-inch diameter polythene tubes, hanging in greenhouses and with a drip-feed watering arrangement. It's called **Vertistrawb**. It is sold as a kit and is said to crop for over six months in the year.

For conventional strawberries, you can sow seed in boxes in January onwards, planting out in the spring, or establish new plants from old by pricking out runners. An average plant will give off several of these. Allow them to root down—either one plant from each runner for big berries or as many as they will take for a clump producing small berries. Cloches will protect them in the spring (with Alpines, this isn't necessary) and they prefer well composted or manured soil, with perhaps a little straw under the plants to keep in moisture and keep the berries clean.

The fruit's best frozen dry, with or without sugar. I've read of one case, again with Alpines, where the seeds have fallen out during freezing and stayed at the bottom of the bag. When they were planted, subsequently, in a covered pot over a radiator, they germinated very quickly and made good plants.

Raspberries are somewhat trickier. We planted a dozen canes each of early and late, called **Orion** and **Promise**, which certainly began well until the weird weather of 1975 first drowned and then baked them. We're still waiting to test their full value.

Raspberries can be planted singly, surrounded by wire attached to a strong post, or in clumps, with longer wire and more posts. Generally, however, they're more convenient in

60

rows, some four or five feet apart and the canes two feet from each other. Dig a trench and manure it, plant and firm in the canes, and then cut them back to about a foot high, to give you strong, young shoots for the next season. Taut wire at two-, three- and five-feet heights, is necessary for support and containment. As the plants mature, you will aim, ideally, for about six canes to each plant. Take off any weak ones and, after fruiting, completely cut out the old wood which bore the fruit. Healthy roots will send out plenty of suckers and these are perfectly good for starting off new plants.

The best planting time is in the late autumn to March, and it's sensible to take the advice of your nursery about varieties, both for taste and fruiting time. Obviously it's better to have a succession of fruits rather than the whole lot all at one (possibly inconvenient) time, so several kinds can be planted in a row at varying times.

Other recommended varieties are the **Mallings**, **Lloyd George** and **September**. There's also a miniature variety, **Pynes Royal**—heavy cropping on short canes—but it's not easy to find.

Gooseberries are good value, if you can keep them from the birds, and they can be trained as espaliers, or in hedges, so they don't have to be space-consuming. Plant two-year-old bushes in November, prune them back in March, and they should last for about twenty years.

Redcurrants can also be trained in the same way as gooseberry bushes, or grown just as bushes, and should also be planted in early winter as two-year-olds, about five feet apart. You might prefer **blackcurrants**, which are bushes only, and which need surface manuring in the spring. Black-currants appear on the previous season's growth, and as you will therefore want strong new shoots from the bottom of the bush you should prune back hard on the branches which have fruited. Red (and white) currants, however, fruit on twigs from established branches, like apples.

As to apples, pears and plums, I am not sure these have a place on the allotment unless, as in my case, they're well-established trees forming a hedge which cuts down the wind without affecting the sunlight. If you want to know more about any of these the RHS publication *The Fruit Garden Displayed* is a fine source.

Incidentally, shaping fruit trees (into cordons, espaliers, fans) is not only decorative; you are also pruning, training and opening them into effective shapes so that the fruit can develop to best advantage. The branches are easy to spray and pick, and as their form usually means they must be supported, the trees are better protected against winds. It's a lot more work, but the crops are better and you get a bigger crop over a smaller area.

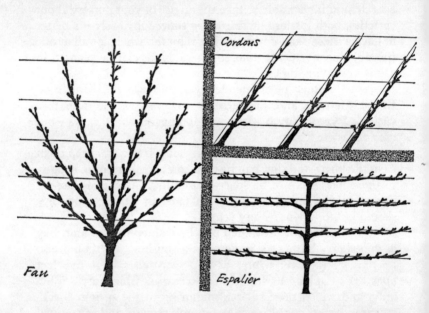

One other fruit I would recommend is the **grape**. There's a very fine one, fruiting heavily, on an allotment near me, and the grapevine does even better in a greenhouse. Keep the vine restricted to two long stems, running to the roof and along underneath it, tied at frequent intervals. The grapes grow on the many side growths from these stems; cut back on excess shoots after the crop is over.

In parenthesis—although it's not strictly an allotment product—you should try making your own wine. Certainly, you can make plenty out of your own fruit, or from pickings you can find in the country or from many flowers. Elderflower wine, for example, is said to be much better than elderberry. I find these country wines take too long fermenting and maturing, whereas the wines we have made from imported concentrated grape juice are drinkable within four weeks of being started. And very drinkable they are, especially if you buy the superior versions with the proper yeasts, and if you have the time, quantity, storage space and patience to let them mature. There are kits and detailed instructions from a number of companies, but we have stayed mainly with the excellent **Southern Vinyards** in Hove. In all cases, however, there is one marvellous thing to be said for the system: it will give you a very acceptable bottle of wine for about a quarter of the price of cheap supermarket plonks.

13 PLAN YOUR PLOT

Plan your plot. A certain amount of paper-work can make the spadework if not easier at least more successful.

Measure your land, translate it to paper, and list precisely what you are growing where, when it is going in and when it is coming out. The following year, you will probably want to move crops around and it's maddening to find that you've forgotten where the previous ones were.

By planning, also, you can ensure constantly available working areas for new planting or for soil preparation.

Crop rotation over a three-year period would mean leaving the permanent sections alone and simply moving the groupings of other plants each season: that is C to B, B to A and A to C, and so on. (Moving the strawberries every few years could be done simply by changing them over with the seedbed or tomato plot. Courgettes are on a ridge.)

Here is how the planned plot might look:

_____ Blackberries _____		
Permanent		
Compost heaps	Tools	Rhubarb
	Raspberries	
Strawberries		Gooseberries and Currants
_____ Raspberries _____		
Rotation		
	Section A	
	Onions	
	Carrots	
	Potatoes	
	Parsnips	
	Beetroot	
	Section B	
	Beans	
	Peas	
	Turnips	
	Leeks	
	Lettuce	
	Celery	
	Section C	
	Cabbage	
	Cauliflower	
	Broccoli	
	Brussels sprouts	
Permanent		
	Seedbed/Cold frame/Tomatoes	
	Courgettes	

You will, according to which vegetable you like, ignore some kinds and give extra space to others. When I began allotment gardening, on a small five-rod plot which in any case was shared, we laid out this plan for our ground:

_____ Sorrel	1 row	_____
_____ Onions	1 row	_____
_____ Shallots	1 row	_____
_____ Carrots	1 row	_____
_____ Lettuce	1 row	_____
_____ Radish (followed by lettuce)	1 row	_____
_____ Broad beans	2 rows	_____
_____ Runner beans	2 rows	_____
Cabbage		Tomatoes
Sprouts		Courgettes
Cauliflower		Compost

On a more recent supplementary plot, broader but still not very long, but one which did not need cultivation for potatoes, cabbages and some other crops, the main plantings and sowings developed like this:

Section A

Onions and Shallots (8 rows)

Radish, carrots, beetroot
and parsnip sown between

Section B

Dwarf French beans (4 rows)

Broad beans (4 rows)

Lettuce (1 row)

Section C

Peas

Tomatoes

Compost

Courgettes

Leeks

Unworked

Runner beans

The amount of unworked land shown in the illustration on page 67 was due to the plot being taken on late and the bad weather of that season then taking over; onions and beans went in first and second simply because that was the first ground to be made ready.

Even so, the root sowings in Section A were a mistake. For one thing, the ground wasn't prepared enough, or deep enough, to give the parsnips and carrots any depth of root, and all of these crops stayed around too long after the onions and beans had been harvested, imposing restrictions on further use of the ground. It was expedient, but bad, planning and its only advantage was that as a result the proper preparation could begin rather earlier than usual for the next season.

Lettuce was mixed with carrot on Section B and this was another mistake because although a mutual thinning had more or less worked there were then two widely separated carrot beds.

Section C was also partly wasted; a compost heap not at the end of a plot breaks up the planting pattern, for one thing.

The plan for the next season looked as below.

As beans leave Section A, brassicas go in. As onions and shallots come out of B, leeks can be transplanted. They will probably have been started in the spare patch.

Section A

French dwarf and early
broad beans (8 rows)

Section B

Onions and shallots (8 rows)
Carrots intersown (3 rows)
Lettuce and radish as
catch-crops

Section C

Broad beans (2 rows)
Peas (3 rows)

Climbing
-French
beans

Climbing
-French
beans

Section D

Tomatoes

Courgettes

Compost

Seedbed/spare

By the autumn, therefore, the whole of Sections A and B should still be growing well, with brassicas, roots and leeks for winter. Section C will be ready for working up and Section D—while still holding on to courgettes and tomatoes for a while—would be the location for the following season's onions and beans.

Having a supplementary plot, by the way, isn't always as good as it sounds, especially if it's on another completely different site. You can't really keep a close eye on both satisfactorily, and there is a lot of fuss and wasted energy entailed in travelling between the two—especially as the tools you need on one are usually still on the other.

14 CALENDAR

More paper-work which can certainly save worry is a simple calendar showing the basics of what to do and when. Usually, I can never remember what I should be doing until it's too late. Make up your own calendar, or use this outline.

JANUARY

Sow broad beans, peas, onion seeds, lettuce. Cover with cloches if it's cold.

Plant shallots (also covered).

Pick brassicas, celery, parsnips, leeks, Jerusalem artichokes as needed.

Order seeds, seed potatoes and onion sets.

Rhubarb should be manured and new roots planted.

Sprinkle lime on new brassica plot and hoe it in.

Cut back raspberry, blackberry, gooseberry and currant bushes.

FEBRUARY

Sow broad beans in the open, at the end of the month, and peas, lettuce, radish, onion, carrots, parsley and, under cloches, summer cabbage.

Plant shallots and Jerusalem artichokes.

Pick parsnips and brassicas.

Start to sprout early potatoes.

Kill couch grass and weeds with dalapon, or paraquat if you're brave and don't have children.

Continue to prune fruit, if necessary.

If you have a greenhouse, sow tomato seed in boxes, ready for transplanting in it in March.

MARCH

Sow cabbage, celery, carrots, leeks, lettuce, peas, radish, sprouts, early potatoes (at the end of the month), onions, parsnips.

Plant last summer's onions, or onion sets, and seedling lettuce under cloches.

Pick the tops of sprouts and turnips.

Use the hoe to kill weeds and to work in a little sodium nitrate (NOT chlorate) around growing cabbages and lettuce.

Train blackberry shoots and complete any fruit pruning.

APRIL

Sow broad beans, beetroot, cabbage, carrots, cauliflower, lettuce, radish, turnips, onions and peas. Also, under cloches, dwarf French beans, runner beans and sweetcorn.

Plant globe artichokes, seedling cauliflowers, and potatoes.

Pick brassicas, early lettuce, radishes, leeks and turnip tops.

Early peas should be showing, so put in sticks. Potato leaves may be showing. If so earth them up, be ready to cover the ridge with straw if there are frosts, and spray against blight.

Weed and hoe.

Order tomato plants.

MAY

Sow beans of any kind, more brassica, and courgettes at the end of the month. More beetroot, carrots, lettuce, radish and turnip, salsify, spinach and sweetcorn.

Plant more sprouts and potatoes.

Thin beetroot, carrots, lettuce, parsnip.

Pick leeks, brassica, salads.

Earth up potatoes.

Hoe and weed.

Mulch peas and beans and plant bean poles.

Dig over cleared ground for autumn crops.

Spray for pests, lay slug pellets.

Cut suckers from fruit bushes.

If it's dry, water copiously and often.

JUNE

Sow beans and peas, beetroot, carrots, lettuce, turnips and swedes.

Plant leeks and tomatoes, late brassicas, courgettes, chicory and celery.

Thin root crops and lettuce.

Pinch out broad bean tops.

Pick salads, beans, peas, brassica and spinach.

Put some protection over fruit bushes against birds.

Hoe, water and spray.

JULY

Sow late peas and beetroot and try late broad beans (you might get a crop). Also turnips, swede and winter radishes.

Plant late brassicas and leeks.

Thin salads, swedes and beetroot.

Pick early potatoes, beetroot and early carrots, peas and beans, summer brassicas, globe artichokes and turnips.

Pick fruit and train new growths.

Pinch out runner bean tops if they're at the tops of poles. Earth up potatoes and sprouts.

Cover cauliflower hearts with leaves.

Tie tomatoes (other than the bush variety) and take off side shoots.

Hoe and weed, water and spray.

AUGUST

Sow next year's onion seeds, autumn and winter lettuce and spring cabbage.

Plant anything green in any space coming free, to fill the winter green gap.

74

Pick anything that looks grown.

Bend down wintered onion tops and lift shallots.

Thin roots if necessary.

Beware holidays: if you're going away, get someone else to pick peas, beans, courgettes. He keeps what he picks and your plants stay fruitful.

Root new strawberries.

Hoe and weed, spray and water.

SEPTEMBER

Sow winter lettuce and turnips (for tops).

Plant winter cabbage.

Bend over spring-planted onion tops and lift them two weeks or so later, to lie and dry.

Pick anything that's ripe. Lift potatoes.

Earth up chicory and celery.

Hoe and water.

OCTOBER

Plant cabbages and winter lettuce.

Earth up celery, leeks, endives.

Pick or lift (for use or storage) sprouts, the last beans, beetroot, early sown carrots, turnips, onions, cabbage, cauliflowers and courgettes.

Dry and burn off dead brassica plants and increase compost heaps.

Start digging old ground for new crops. Hoe anywhere else.

NOVEMBER

Sow next year's (paraffin treated) early broad beans.

Clear your plot, except for winter roots and brassicas.

Dig and manure: at least half of the ground should be available.

DECEMBER

Dig if you still have to, but not if it's wet, soggy and sticky ground. Otherwise, take the month off and leave it all alone.

15 WEEDS, PESTS AND FOODS

Perhaps it all seems a lot that, with the possible exception of December, you are going to be working and slaving the whole year, and when you are not actually working you are thinking about it? But it doesn't have to be constant toil. There are purists' ways of doing things and there are other sloppier but still effective ways.

I can see no sense at all in becoming obsessed with tomatoes and their constant husbandry when I can simply plant a different but very delicious kind and then leave them alone until I can eat them. I can see no sense in going through the dozen or so ways of growing and blanching celery when the self-blanching kind is quicker and easier and—although less hardy—just as tasty.

A lot of the fun in allotment gardening is in finding out what you can get away with, and a lot of the work is made simpler by common sense. Difficulties, on the other hand, come from the mysticism which experts propagate, even if they don't mean to. Perhaps it's that they know so much, and we so little, and it does not occur to them to tell us the basic simplicities.

For example, a woman asked me as I was writing this if I would include a chapter on cold frames, explaining why and how they were used and why—in her case—they were not very successful. She doesn't need a chapter—but, as she said, nobody had appeared to tell her anything in the books she had read, or in the broadcasts she had heard. Her only reason for having cold frames was to keep the woodpigeons away from some things in her garden.

My main reason for using glass is to provide a sort of overcoat for delicate young plants going out into the crisp spring air, or to allow a bit of extra sun on slower plants which need to catch up. But nobody had told her, either, that if you shut up plants in a glass box they will be deprived of air, water and perhaps some kind of natural immunity so that you must open the frames, some of the time, to provide this, and water the plants more often, and gradually let the young things out into the open without their coats in case they wilt from too much heat.

As with frames, so with cloches. She found hers expensive and damaging. But if you make a tunnel of cloches, *don't* let it become a wind tunnel—and *do* expect to have to water what's in it more often and more carefully. And if, as in her case, the main reason for a cloche was to keep off pigeons, a simpler protection and one much cheaper is to spread lines of strong thread between half-discs of wood, firmly set into the ground.

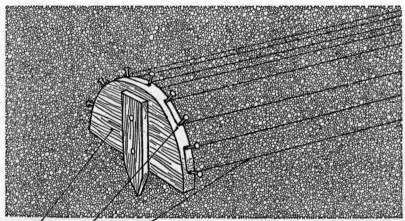

Wood   Nails   Strong thread

I don't dig my allotment as often as some people do—in part, because I don't always have the time and inclination, in part because I'm not totally persuaded it's necessary. When I've had no chance of making a uniform fine tilth, I've grown perfectly acceptable plants in rough ground by making pockets of sieved topsoil, compost and peat where I need it.

We rarely use sprays, partly on ecological grounds, partly because I'm lazy, and partly because they're expensive. Often I can't remember which plants should have what—and also my plants generally seem to do fairly well on their own, expecially with a little help from their friends.

Of whom the finest is the ladybird. My wife collects them where she sees them, and relocates them equally between beans and her roses at home. They keep the greenfly and black-fly down very well and it would be unkind to kill them off, as well, with a spray.

I'm less bothered than some of my neighbours about clearing away nettles, just for the sake of the ladybirds. Nettles attract green-fly, and I'd rather they were there than anywhere else. Green-fly attract ladybirds and everyone prospers except the green-fly.

But if you must use insecticides, the systemic kind are very effective. The chemical gets inside the plant, kills off what aphids are on it and creates a reserve against new ones coming along. They work on the same principle as fire-proofing. And systemic fungicides and fertilisers are also available.

Whether you spray or not, it is as well, I suppose, that you be aware of the most common weeds and pests, and what to do about them.

Weeds are the simplest, especially if they're annual. It is mostly a matter of pulling them out or hoeing them down. If they are not seeding, I let mine lie where they fall, providing a green mulch which helps to keep in moisture. As they dry and rot, they gradually work into the ground, adding humus. I'm not convinced it matters all that much if they are seeding, for any plot of land harbours millions of weed seeds and some are bound to germinate and start new weeds as the ground is turned.

The worst of the weeds are perennials. For example, bramble, which is easier killed by chemicals than by pulling out; bindweed, whose roots and surface growth spread alarmingly if you leave it; ground elder, which is just as bad;

creeping buttercup; thistle and dandelion, ribwort and couch grass. They are all nuisances and I rate couch grass as the worst.

One neighbour recommends rough digging up to three times when—he says—couch grass will then give in. It's not my experience—and anyway, I've never had the time and space to give a plot that kind of working over. I believe the best answer is to dig up every bit of the white, tenuous root. Dalapon is however a guaranteed killer of this and other perennials.

There are three basic chemical weedkillers.

Selective chemicals (like dalapon) kill some plants while ignoring others. Read the instructions carefully.

Total weedkillers (like paraquat, sodium chlorate) explain themselves. They are dangerous to people (and nobody, as I write, has yet found a way of stopping paraquat killing people) and you may also be unable to use the soil for a varying period after using some of them. Again, read the instructions carefully.

Pre-emergence killers are for spraying on bare ground. They destroy weed seeds but not the plant seeds, unless you overdo the amounts.

I'd still rather hoe. For one thing, this gets air and water and warmth to the roots of vegetables, which therefore do better. And some weeds will be kept down simply by being smothered—say, by bush tomatoes, potatoes, marrows—or by crop rotation.

Pests are more complicated and, often of course, are harboured and encouraged by weeds if you let weeds develop. The list is enormous and the responsive agents almost as many. Here are a few of what some of your plants might face, and how to fight them.

Beans. *Black-fly*: pinch out broad bean tops once the plants have flowered and spray with malathion or dust with derris. Watch out for *slugs*—when you will use slug pellets.

Cabbage, etc. *Root-fly*: this gives swollen roots and rotten cabbages as the maggots eat their way upwards. If you've got it, dig up the plants and burn them and don't put any more brassicas there for a while. *Club root* (more common): protect against this (and root-fly) by keeping the soil limed, dipping roots into calomel or BHC powder when planting, and dusting the soil with calomel or soaking it with lindane. *Cabbage white butterfly*: catch it in the egg stage, by spraying with malathion or derris, under the leaves and in their folds. Sprays generally only kill what they hit.

Carrots. *Carrot-fly*: dust with BHC when sowing. Plant near onions, which will also gain protection from BHC, against onion-fly. If either plant is affected, burn it and don't plant more of the same in the same area for a season.

Potatoes. *Scab*: dig in more manure (or perhaps less lime) next time, and it shouldn't happen. *Green skins*: earth them up better. *Blight*: copper sprays if the leaves start showing dark patches and rot. The affected leaves should be burned.

Peas. *Pea moth*: Spray with BHC or derris when the peas are flowering. This is a precaution, really, because you probably won't know you've got the pest until you find maggots in the pods, but peas started in pots and transplanted are usually immune from this anyway.

Celery. *Celery-fly*: destroy the brown-blistered leaves and spray with malathion. Watch out for the same pest in **parsnips**.

Lettuce. *Green-fly*: apply ladybirds. Spray if you must, but well before picking and eating.

Turnips and **swedes.** *Flea-beetle*: BHC and plenty of watering. This pest, which makes small holes in the leaves, thrives only in dry weather.

Tomatoes. *Blight*: copper sprays.

Fruit: a tar-based spray in winter and a derris spray in spring protect apples, pears and plums against *aphids*. Derris and fungicide mixed together are worth applying during and after blossom time. A fungicide is useful against mildew on blackcurrants and gooseberries, and derris can stop the raspberry beetle enjoying your raspberries before you do. A malathion and fungicide mixed spray can help strawberries against aphids and mould, but not after flowering.

Generally, then, a few basic pest-killers are all you need—BHC, malathion or derris, a copper spray, and a fungicide. Club root powder (used as a powder or as a paste) you can usually buy at your allotment society.

There are, besides, some basic foods well worth applying to the ground. One is lime enjoyed by most plants, except potatoes. But don't overdo it, for it can take years to work out if too much is added to the soil. Nitrogen is essential, as are phosphate and potash. Nitrogen grows leaves, phosphates grow roots and potash grows fruit and hardens the plants. All three come in manures and composts, but small additions to some particular plants are useful. A surface dressing of all three in February to April, hoed or forked in, will help the plot generally. And if the old men in the allotment shed want to sell you dried blood and fish meal and bone meal and all other manners of things, why not, *if* you feel like it.

16 FURTHER READING

Because I've tried to design this as a guide to beginners, amateurs, incompetents and corner-cutters, I hope you won't need many other books. Certainly there is a vast library to choose from and its scope deters me. So I shan't even try to recommend any, other than the very few which are on my (wife's) garden shelf.

First of all, and less as a practical guide than as inspirational material, are two by John Seymour called *The Fat of the Land* and *Self-Sufficiency*. Both are now published in paperback by Faber, though each is worth the hardback price. For, cranky though some have regarded him, John Seymour has a vast, ebullient talent for transmitting enthusiasm and a huge and successful experience of living on what he has grown. It was from reading the first of his books that I developed my own enthusiasm for growing vegetables.

A collection of three books reprinted by David and Charles is also, though not cheap, well worth having and again inspirational garden literature. They are written by the late E. A. Bowles—*My Garden in Spring, My Garden in Summer* and *My Garden in Autumn and Winter*.

In practical terms, two Royal Horticultural Society publications, *The Vegetable Garden Displayed* and *The Fruit Garden Displayed* are well worth looking at. There are two excellent books by Reader's Digest—*The Gardening Year* and, much more comprehensive and perhaps less necessary in day-to-day use, the *Encyclopaedia of Garden Plants and Flowers*. Companionable and handy is the Fontana paperback *The Sunday Gardener*, edited by Professor Alan Gemmell.

Look also at Loewenfeld and Back's paperback,

Herbs for Health and Cookery (Pan), Richard Mabey's Fontana paperback, *Food for Free*, and *Freeze Now, Dine Later* by Althaus and ffrench-Hodges (Faber).

In addition ten pence will be well spent every Tuesday on a copy of *Garden News*.

POSTSCRIPT

Such a plot must have a woman in it

S. Richardson

My wife required of me that this book should appear to have nothing to do with her. It's an expression of her disbelief that I could get it right. She's also afraid that her fellow-students at a class where they are working for an RHS Diploma in Horticulture might thus identify and blame her.

Well, I may not indeed have got it right by professional standards—but it works for me. And she, good cook that she is, also gets a better product for her cooking at a saving of several pounds a month.

When I began growing vegetables it was on the understanding that she was the expert and I the common labourer. What she directed, so would I do. But although I am still mocked as the man who planted her tradescantia upside down some years ago, I've learned more about growing than I would ever have thought possible—a lot of it by trial and error, a lot of it by common sense, and by watching and listening to other people.

If you, too, are beginning as I began, you should develop just as effectively. Probably more so.

And at least you will be helping yourself survive in these inflated seventies.

GLOSSARY

Acid

Soil with less than 7·0 pH content. Don't worry about defining that; all you need to know is that 7·0 is neutral on this pH scale, that below it is acid soil and above, alkaline. Acid soil is deficient in lime. Therefore, lime-loving plants like the brassicas don't do well in it unless lime is added.

Aeration

Stirring up the soil to let air get to the roots.

Alkaline

(See Acid.) Shouldn't cause trouble to vegetables.

Annual

Plant that grows and dies within a year.

Aphid

A common pest or blight—green-fly, black-fly the fruit tree's woolly aphis and many others—which needs thorough spraying with malathion or a systemic insecticide. This is a pest poison sprayed on to the plant, which ingests it; the plant itself is not harmed but aphids on it will be.

Blanched

Leaves (say, of celery) where light's been kept away by covering them with pots, cardboard tubes, slate, or earth.

Bolted

As when, say, what should have been a football-shaped lettuce has grown upwards instead and it now looks more like a Chinese pagoda. It's run to seed too soon, probably because of overcrowding or poor ground or not enough water.

Brassicas

Cabbages and their close relatives—sprouts, broccoli, cauliflower, kale. They're all prone

87

to club-root. Protect against this fungus by dusting the soil with lime and calomel.

Catch-crop A quick one: sown, grown and cleared again between or alongside longer-term crops. Radish or lettuce, for example.

Clamp A 'natural' store for potatoes and other roots: they're laid on straw, covered with more straw, and then covered again with earth. It must be firmed, ventilated and drained.

Cloche Usually a 'tent' made of glass (or plastic) sheets, for bringing on early plants or poor starters. Was once a bell-shaped glass cover, hence the French name. Can nowadays be a polythene tunnel.

Club Root See Aphid.

Cold Frame A kind of low, mini-greenhouse, with rising or sliding glass top, for starting off tender plants or giving them extra warmth or humidity.

Compost Organic waste carefully collected and compressed and encouraged to rot until it forms a rich, easily broken food to be dug into or spread on the ground. Compost is usually vegetable matter (see Manure). Also a kind of seeding and potting compound sold commercially: the best known are the John Innes varieties for different uses.

Cordon When apples, pears or certain soft fruits are trained on the single main stem of the plant.

Curd The white 'head' of cauliflower (or broccoli). It is, in fact, a flower bud.

Dibber A thick pointed stick for making holes for transplanting. Sometimes called a dibble.

Drill A shallow furrow, flat-bottomed or V-shaped, for seed-planting.

Earthed up   As for celery (see Blanched) or potatoes. Soil is drawn up round the stems or leaves of certain plants to deprive them of light.

Espalier   Fruit trees trained with a very few branches from the main stem and which are horizontally opposed.

Friable   The nature of soil when it's soft and crumbly. When the surface of this is raked it becomes fine-grained and good for seed-planting. This is known as a tilth.

Fungicide   Kills fungus (mostly found on fruit trees). It will probably be a copper-based spray.

Germination   A seed's first stage in becoming a plant, usually by reaction with moisture.

Hardening   A process of acclimatising tender young plants to the open as the days get warmer. It's done under glass with gradually more and more exposure to the open.

Hardy   Plants which are generally resistant to the British winter.

Half-hardy   Plants which aren't.

Humus   The final product of good compost, the 'body' which goes into the ground.

Lime   Often needed in moderate amounts to balance certain soils. See Acid.

Manure   Fertiliser. It is mostly animal excreta, bone or blood, probably mixed with straw or some other vegetation, and breaks down to humus for feeding the soil. See Compost. It can also be bought in concentrated liquid form. **Green manure** is a crop specially grown for digging into and enriching the soil, such as mustard or rape or clover.

Mulch   A surface layer, usually of compost or manure, which helps to preserve moisture for plants, to feed them and to suppress weeds around them. A **dust mulch** is a layer of fine dry soil for keeping the moisture below ground.

Peat   Decayed bog vegetation which adds humus to soils.

Perennial   Plant that does not die within the year but which, after its dormant period, revives for a number of years.

Pinched out   Taking off the tops (or branches) of certain plants (say broad beans for tops or most tomatoes for branches) to restrict plant growth and promote fruit growth.

Potted   When plants with their soil are put into their permanent pots, this is potting-**up**. When they're moved into bigger pots to allow more growth, this is potting-**on**. When pots are changed *for* a change, after some years, this is **re**-potting.

Pricked out   When seedlings (or rooted cuttings) are first planted out.

Pruning   Cutting back the growth of plants, either for shape or for more fruit.

Rotation   Planting crops of the same kind in different places in successive years, to 'rest' the ground and improve the yield.

Runner   A branch (say of a strawberry or blackberry) which can take root where it touches the ground.

Spit   The depth of a spade blade, or the depth of soil which will normally be dug by a spade.

Sucker   An extra stem from the roots of an established plant. Usually undesirable.

Systemic   See Aphid.

Tilth   See Friable.

Top-dressing   Mulching, but usually for pot plants and by the replacement of the top inch or so of soil or potting compost with a fresh layer.

Trench   Usually at least a foot wide and a spit deep, heavily manured and re-filled, for planting certain crops.

Truss   A bunch of tomato fruits on a side-shoot.

INDEX